A World of Octobers

Scarlett Olacsi

BookLeaf Publishing

India | USA | UK

Presentation by *BookLeaf Publishing*

Web: www.bookleafpub.com

E-mail: info@bookleafpub.com

ISBN: 9789358317756

First edition 2023

DEDICATION

While I have many people I love in this world, I cannot dedicate this book to all of them. Rather, I'd like to dedicate to someone I've struggled to love but have been through so much with. Scarlett - we've finally made it, love. Keep going always.

ACKNOWLEDGEMENT

I'd like to thank BookLeaf publishing for this wonderful opportunity. I'd also like to thank my family - Mom, Dad, Michael, Austin, Jake - you've made me who I am today. I will always be grateful to you.
Additionally, I want to express my appreciation to my Aunt Sarah - you've always supported my dreams. If there's any adult I trusted growing up, it was you. You were always a safe place for me. I love you.
Lastly, I'd like to thank my best friends. Tracer, I wouldn't have made it this far without you. Athena, you've always believed in me. I know my friends are proud of me and that is so important. I'm lucky to have you. May you live a life of wonderful Octobers.

PREFACE

This is the 18th October of my life, and as always, a blend of fall shades color my world as I stare above at the October skies. Leaves rustle above me, the wind starts to howl, the night becomes darker, and the days more beautiful. If I wrote a poem everyday in October, each one would be a singular depth into my life as I've grown, perhaps faster then I would have liked. My life has been full of extraordinary Octobers. This world has been full of extraordinary Octobers.

October Worlds

I watch summer die
A corpse of October left behind
And I have never doubted Autumn's beauty
A soft pumpkin palette
Subdued colors
Every so often hit with a brilliant brightness
Of a scarlet sunset
Saturated orange juice
Dripping down the sky -
Then it leaves the earth
In a copper goodbye. . .
Maybe there's more October evenings in you
Then all the nights combined
Perhaps there are more
October worlds
In this brilliant multiverse
Then I thought, before.

October Morning

I wake one October morning
A cool wind flushes my cheeks
And bites at my nose
If I were to stay in bed
I would waste
This beautiful moment
Poetic in its own individuality
I would write a thousand poems
If I could stay
In an October morning -
Leaves of purple
Red, orange, and yellow
Ripened to the cursed autumn
I've never seen a death
So beautiful
October suns
Shine down on my summer stained cheeks
I can't help but think of the blackberries
Growing over the fence
At the park behind
Your house
We used to watch the leaves shimmer
Used to watch the birds fly south
And when the first frost comes
I hope it freezes over my fingers

So I may be stuck in an October morning
Of nostalgia, of memory
Of hope, of brilliance
For a few eons more

Blue Denim

I listen to your insights
Taking note of every articulation
You speak like a writer,
And I've always been a reader.
From classical literature
To modern fiction
To romance
The words fly off the page and create a legend in
my brain
I hear you talk and suddenly I can see a future
Long nights in the library
Coffee shops, bookstores
I see a vision
So clearly by your side
It is not perfect,
But it is raw
It is new
I've been searching for a place to begin
Drone on for hours, I will listen
Send me the paragraph
The essay
The book
I'll annotate and write notes in the margins for
you
I'll highlight my favorite parts

And learn it by heart
Be the story I finally enter
Let me be the character you keep by your side
Let me color in the illustrations
And turn black and white pages
Into a parade of colors
Starting with eyes
Of blue denim.

Regular

I told myself I wouldn't write a sad poem
It's easy to feel like a failure
When you're doing your best
And still don't get it right
But I've had teachers call me smart, insightful
I was offended once by a girl who had read more
books then I did
She had time
I spend my time wastefully
I could be trying harder
I thought I was trying harder -
I once decided I was unbreakable
If I hurt, I'd pick up the pieces and trudge on
I've always kept going, kept living, kept showing
up
But I'm not who I thought I would be
By now
The truth is my story is not interesting
The truth is I'm not a fairytale or a tragedy either
I am simply regular
I try to study to become something
I try to write my experiences into poetry
But the truth is I am not unbreakable
I am breaking down
Most of the time.

I thought I'd be better by now
People leave but I always kept going
Now I stand here with 48 staircases
To go till the next floor
And then thousands more after that
To get to the top
I told myself I wouldn't write a sad poem
I think misery is just so close of a friend of mine
That I can't help falling back into its arms
Time and time again
My story is not fit for a movie
Or a play
Or a book -
It's just regular
My voice stays quiet in the beats behind bruises
and ticks of the clock
I'm not who I thought I would be by now
I was close to becoming a classic novel once
But then the main character took a final look at
me and said
You're not who I thought you would be
By now

My Favorite Color

Why have you hidden
These colors all year?
I'm not sure I understand
Where all this gold and red has come from
The flowers have turned to leaves and they
dance in the wind
I remember orange marigolds
Now I see acorns scattered across the lawn
Fallen
Shades of autumn
I think my favorite color
Is October
You've revealed
The hues inside you
You've hidden them so long
I think everyone has an October
I think my favorite color
is you.

First Frost

After the first frost, I inspect a line of small
pumpkins at the market
I notice fall leaves and winter coats as I walk
across campus
Sorrow seems to swell and blend in with the
scent of morning dew and burning pine
Apple cider and pumpkin spice are now perfume
scents and lotions
I pull an orange cardigan over me -
The trees are dying. The birds have left.
It should be sad,
But once upon an October,
When the last day comes
Ghosts and ghouls
Come out to play
And i get to dance with those
I've missed
For a very long time.

its 12 a.m and I can't think of a title

I work from 10:30 a.m to 5 p.m
I study in all places whether it be a car, a desk,
or under an autumn tree
I'm always putting this pressure on myself
To be the best I can be
Still, my assignments don't seem to always be
on time
I write and work and study but I feel incomplete
My brain is an egg
Cracked onto a pan over a burning stove
It's frying and burning and the yolk is spilling
out -
I just want a day
Where I don't have to be better than anyone else
A day where I can feel free
From the burdens that weigh on my shoulders
I carry the textbooks
Piles of paper and ink
It'll pay off, I tell myself
I can push through
Dreams don't make themselves
I've been taught to work for what I want -
If you want to be successful
If you want to achieve anything

One day I'll look back and be glad, right?
Glad that I didn't take a break
Other than to write a poem or two
One day I'll look back, right?
And think that it was worth it.

Schoolgirl Crush

I've made it so far
Then my eyes fall on him
Thought loving was a waste of time
But I'd be okay if he wasted mine
Think I met him once in a dream
Think we passed by each other suddenly
But I never would've remembered his name
If he hadn't spoke in rhymes

Know it's only been a week
But he listens when I speak
He doesn't quote anybody else
And God he speaks in poetry

I take note of the signs
And I memorize the lines
I have such a interesting mind
That it's easy to fantasize

Give me a glance
Give me a chance
Just look in my eyes then I'll teach you to dance
If you'd be my best friend
I will be yours
I'll stay up with you for hours

We'll open all the doors
I'll write you a constellation
If you just would look at my stars
It would be a nice sensation
The world would be ours
Don't misunderstand
I know what I'm worth
But if I write the line
Could you help me make it rhyme?
I'll start the verse
Love isn't a curse
And I'm going on a whim here
This is something I can't rehearse
But together we could write a story
Let our lives intertwine
for a chapter or two
Or the rest of time
If you really wouldn't mind
You could choose to be mine

Blue

My eyes are blue like the ocean
Like waves that pull you under and spit you out
Her eyes are blue like the sky
Like paper airplanes floating down
Like clouds and balloons
His eyes are blue like the evening
Dark fades to light
Golden sunset lights up the sky
Our eyes are blue like
Poetry

Mosaic of Blue Patterns

I looked into a new friends eyes the other day
I thought his eyes were of blue denim
And then I thought of the evening skies
A song I memorized and never forgot
I had a best friend when I was 12
She was a know it all, a bad influence
My mom didn't like her
But her eyes were soft like a baby blue sky
They always made me melt
Like ice cream in the sun
I had a dream the other night
I was dressed as the little red riding hood again.
But instead of seeing a monstrous wolf
I saw a kid
With eyes of shallow water
I think blue eyes have always meant something
to me
I look in the mirror, inside the raging deep
oceans contained in a vessel of a girl
It's always been blue
But when people tell me
They see hints of green
When I look into my mother's golden ring
planets she calls eyes
I start to feel a little less familiar

And a little more like I matter
I think this isn't quite fair to blue
blue is a light that I always found
But then wished it would get lost for me
Just so I wouldn't have to remember
For awhile
But the truth is, it's a pretty color.
The truth is forgiveness is like the color blue.
Whether it's denim jean dreams
Or the nostalgic evening blue skies
Baby blue with clouds painted
Like cotton balls on construction paper -
Blue eyes of shallow water
That emptiness as I become numb
The oceans of my eyes -
Are always filling with different shades
Of mosaic blue patterns.

Forest of Paper and Ink

All my poems suddenly seem inadequate
I turn through the pages trying to find one
That isn't about someone else
That isn't about being miserable,
A poem with metaphors that turn your thoughts
into proses
Your fingers into quill and ink pens
A poem that isn't about love
But the words only ever come from the confines
of my heart
They rhyme unevenly like the beats in my chest
I know I've written about myself before
About tears of apple seeds
That grow into trees of poetry
A forest of novels
The morning dew on the leaves
Drip into my mouth in a drought
I gather them up in jars and vials
In hopes to water my garden
So there will be nourishment next summer
I watch the vines grow over me in an arch of
cucumbers and green beans
Herbs start to fill my nose with hints of
rosemary and thyme in the bathtub
I take a tomato

As if I were a child going hungry
But somehow when I bite though, it is hollow
inside
Plants do not always grow the way you expect
them too
To tell you the truth, I have not grown in the way
I thought I would
18, finally free, and still I labor as my flowers
wilt
None of my poetry
Dew drops on leaves of green
Seemed to be good enough
So I stand barefoot in the grass
When by some miracle
It begins to rain
There are no songbirds to sing for me
But I have stopped clipping the thorns off my
roses
I will grow
But wildflowers like me
Bloom more than once
Like dandelion yellow
Becomes white fluff
A weed that people wish upon
I will grow into a sanctuary
As the squash
The bell peppers
The jalapenos feed the mouths
Of starving artists

As I use the earth
To create more lines
For my forest of
Paper and ink.

Autumn

I am the daughter of / falling leaves / of
beautiful death. / Of flowers, summer rain / I
have been compared to Persephone / a goddess
of spring / and the underworld / I am the soft
colors / of rebirth / hope / I am the creek that
flows in my small town/I am the metal bridge
that echoes as you walk across / I am a few steps
behind from the group / lost in the scenery / I am
the light that got lost / I am the darkness of a
night sky / I am the moon / constantly changing /
phases of / light / and stars / listen. I have so
much to say / and a quiet voice / there are people
who need me / alone, unhappy / and I am too /
my English teacher says / you can always start
over / so I go to sleep / and hibernate / until a
new chance comes / a rebirth, a spring / of
crawdads / and swallows / of snipes / forgotten/
and therefore / non existent. Of bird songs / of
dark rooms / different songs but same notes /
bring me forward / in memory / never forget / or
I'll become a legend / I am the daughter of /
Persephone /naive and / grown.

A World of Octobers

Poetry books and pumpkins fill my little autumn
room
I try to gather the leaves and create crowns to sit
atop the heads of my stuffed animals
I fill the space with fall scented candles and fairy
lights
Call me a daughter of Demeter
My sister Persephone has left
And brought about my turn to shine -
I am autumn
I am the wind upon your cheeks
Even the sun steps away from me
To allow the trees to bask
Under scorpio stars
They paint their leaves
The colors in my hair
Apple red, glittering gold, and pumpkin orange
Allow me to stand above your northern
hemisphere
Let the shade of my shadow bring about your
halloween night
If it were my way
This world would be
A world of Octobers.

Home

I used to watch golden leaves flutter in the wind
I used to watch the birds go by in the sky
Flying south, i presume
I fell in love with the leaves I tread on
colors below my feet
The crunching sound they make when I step on
them
I used to lay under blackberry fences
I remember walking home from school one day
In the rain
I was depressed at the time of this beauty
But it was bright and I am in love
With the way
You used to hold my hand
I am in love
Though life is kinder now
It's weird how sometimes you miss
Things that weren't right for you
The leaves turn from green to gold
To reds, oranges
Life changes and so have I
I fell in love with an autumn whisper
Of the wind that takes me
Home.

The Right Thing *mention of suicide*

I haven't seen the sunset in awhile
Trying to shed my problems like trees do to the
dying leaves
One of my best friends texted me yesterday at 10
pm
Do you want to kill yourself with me?
October was meant to be sweet and sticky on my
tongue
It is heavy like maple syrup
It is heavy and I am trying to do the right things
The right thing was probably not what I did,
But it relieved you,
So I don't mind being the angel
With a shotgun from now on
One of my best friends asked me
Could you at least hold me while I die?
I wish to dance around the past
Ghosts of my voice and the things I once offered
I am trying to do the right thing
The sun goes down and in my dreams I am
holding you as the breath escapes from your
lungs
I am unable to get out of bed when the
nightmare ends

I am stuck on the sheets
I feel heavy, weak
I'm trying to do the right thing
But i have made mistakes
October is heavy
I wish to shed my problems like trees do
To the dying leaves -
I want the world to fall away
But I am trying to do the right thing
So I send the text
So I stay up as long as I can
So I pray to a God I've never believed in
Or rather, I pray to October
Please let them smile
Once more.

A day in my life

A can of caffeinated liquid
Tastes like peach rings and sugar
I wear an orange cardigan and an orange skirt
like a pumpkin
Complete with a little green beret
Today in Lit we ate pizza
My 3 o'clock class was canceled
Now I sit around in the ILC building
Or explore around campus
My days go like this
They start to blur together, even though I enjoy
them
Essay after assignment after project
I put in my two weeks at the sandwich shop
So I can focus on academia
Halloween parties start next week and I have yet
to ruin my white dress
Splatters of blood
It is October
My life is going
It goes and goes and goes and I ride along
I enjoy the fall colors
the way my pastel rainbow converse look in a
pile of red, gold, and purple leaves
It is my world

In October
Call me a peach or call me your little pumpkin
I appreciate the festivity
Life goes on and on and on and on
I talk to you sometimes in my dreams
I used to regret it
But I don't think I do anymore
I may hold on inside
But does letting go really mean forgetting
I haven't forgotten
What October used to look like
So I make new memories
Life goes on and on and on
I live a normal life,
I always wished for life to be kinder to me
But really all I needed was for me to be kinder to
myself.

Pumpkin Patch

The fire stains my hair with red
It is of candy apples
Of candy canes
And we could wander the pumpkin patch
together
We could find the biggest one together
Take it home and carve it into something we like
Then light a flame inside it
Watch it glow in dark
watch the spark burn inside
And maybe life is a little like pumpkins
maybe we can carve it into something we like
maybe we can light a fire
Let it color us in sunsets and red licorice
I would hold your hand
In the patch -
But we don't have to
We can walk around
Forward, back, all the way around
Doesn't matter to me
As long as we keep searching
For the roundest one
That we can stick a knife in
and create a face with
triangle eyes

Or we could sit by the pond
or on the wooden swing
our hands around hot cups of cider
Doesn't matter to me
As long as you and I
Make a memory
That we can carry
All the way home
Together.

Different

I could put on my orange cardigan
and green beret
I could zip up a striped hoodie
or wear pants half pink half black
Plaid skirts
Dresses with a pattern of
Black bats over pink fabric
The trees are golden over us
I could sit here and talk with strangers
I could study until I fall asleep
It's October
And there is no shortage
Of styles
Of ways to survive
I smell the rain in the air
I crunch on the leaves beneath my feet
And become someone different
Every day
Every new thing
I put on.

Everything But You

Pink and purple clouds bloom in the light blue
sky
I can see the town's water tower against it
We were just kids in the backseat
In the grocery market's parking lot -
We walked the streets of our once small town
And now we're 18
I'm in college
And though I know you see my posts online
Though I know you already see my success
My fun -
I wish I could tell you to your face
I made it
I really made it
I walk the campus sidewalks
Gold and red leaves rain onto us
And I love my current friends just as much
But once upon a time
We were kids in the backseat
In the high school parking lot
Blasting music, drinking coffee and energy
drinks
We were kids once
I still see the youth in you
Though we never talk

Maybe someday when the wounds are older
We'll run into each other
At the gas station we used to walk to
Maybe I'll tell you then
I made it
I made it
I got everything I wanted.
Everything
Other than the promise we made
When we were 16.
Everything
Everything but you.

Let Go

Fall has always been about letting go
I try to delete your contact off my phone but I
can't seem to find the courage
What if you call me one day
But it's not saved in my phone
With your name at the top
And I don't answer.
I tell myself I will never go back to how things
used to be
I watch the people around me fall for the same
things I used to
I watch him forgive over and over
I used to be like that once
Now I give him the advice I would've given
younger me
Let go, Let go, Let go
Block them
You can forgive but never forget
I want to tell them, Stay away from him
But unfortunately, we cannot make decisions for
our friends or family
So instead I take my old advice
I stop waiting
I start living
I let go

Let go, let go, let go
You will be missing all your life
Might as well start making new memories
You'll be missing
New friends
New experiences
And the more things you pile on
The less you'll remember the stuff at the bottom
So I let go, let go, let go.

Can you walk?

Dead leaves gather around my feet
The more I stand still
The more the trees I stand under
The more colorful the ground gets
And I start to gather them all up
I will make a pile, and I will jump
When I was 6 years old
I jumped in a leaf pile and landed on my back
I ended up in the ER
I remember coloring books and crayons
I faintly remember a man asking me if I could
walk
12 years later I walk around the city of trees
The dead things get stuck in my hair
So I ride the wind
And hope eventually they blow away
When I was 14
I made a pile outside the seminary building
I was waiting for you
So we could jump together
Even if I landed on my knees
I didn't mind bruises much back then
4 years later
It feels like forever ago and yesterday at the
same time

I stand in front of the leaf pile
The autumn weather starts to scatter them and I
Am still standing here
It feels like I'm still right where
You left me
It feels like there is someone standing over me
Asking, can you walk?
So I breathe in the crisp air
And I jump in
I land on my feet and sigh in relief
I faintly remember a man asking me if I could
walk
So I step forward and let the wind push me
forward
I am
Blowing away
I am
Letting go
I am
Speaking
Yes, yes, sir
I can walk.

www.ingramcontent.com/pod-product-compliance
Lightning Source LLC
LaVergne TN
LVHW051240200726

843510LV00011B/1622